WHEN TROUBLE COMES!

Sermons For Sundays
After Pentecost (Last Third)
Cycle B, First Lesson Texts

Zan W. Holmes, Jr.

CSS Publishing Company, Inc., Lima, Ohio

WHEN TROUBLE COMES!

Copyright © 1996 by
CSS Publishing Company, Inc.
Lima, Ohio

All rights reserved. No part of this publication may be reproduced in any manner whatsoever without the prior permission of the publisher, except in the case of brief quotations embodied in critical articles and reviews. Inquiries should be addressed to: Permissions, CSS Publishing Company, Inc., P.O. Box 4503, Lima, Ohio 45802-4503.

Scripture quotations are from the *New Revised Standard Version of the Bible*, copyright 1989 by the Division of Christian Education of the National Council of the Churches of Christ in the USA. Used by permission.

Library of Congress Cataloging-in-Publication Data

When trouble comes : sermons for the Sundays after Pentecost (last third), cycle B, first lesson texts / Zan W. Holmes.
    p.   cm.
Includes bibliographical references.
ISBN 0-7880-0785-8 (pbk.)
   1. Church year sermons. 2. Bible. O.T.—Sermons. 3. United Methodist Church (U.S.)—Sermons. 4. Methodist Church—United States—Sermons. I. Title.
BX8333.H5854W47   1996
252'.076—dc20   96-20273
                                                                                  CIP

This book is available in the following formats, listed by ISBN:
   0-7880-0785-8   Book
   0-7880-0786-6   IBM 3 1/2
   0-7880-0787-4   Mac
   0-7880-0788-2   Sermon Prep

PRINTED IN U.S.A.

This book is dedicated to all my students who taught me more about preaching than I have taught them.

Likewise, I dedicate this book to all the members of my congregation who have given me helpful feedback that has fed me forward in my ministry of preaching.

Table Of Contents

Introduction   7

Proper 22   9
Pentecost 20
Ordinary Time 27
    When Trouble Comes!
    Job 1:1; 2:1-10

Proper 23   15
Pentecost 21
Ordinary Time 28
    When We Feel God Has Moved And Left No
        Forwarding Address
    Job 23:1-9, 16-17

Proper 24   19
Pentecost 22
Ordinary Time 29
    We Can't Contain God In Our Cups!
    Job 38:1-7 (34-41)

Proper 25   23
Pentecost 23
Ordinary Time 30
    It Came To Pass
    Job 42:1-6, 10-17

Proper 26   27
Pentecost 24
Ordinary Time 31
    From Singleness To Solidarity
    Ruth 1:1-18

All Saints' Sunday   33
    Guess Who's Coming To Dinner?
    Isaiah 25:6-9

Proper 27   37
Pentecost 25
Ordinary Time 32
    From Rejection To Redemption
    Ruth 3:1-5; 4:13-17

Proper 28   41
Pentecost 26
Ordinary Time 33
    When The Odds Are Against Us
    1 Samuel 1:4-20

Christ The King   45
    From The Redemption Of A King To A King Of Redemption
    2 Samuel 23:1-7

Thanksgiving Day   49
    When It's Hard To Give Thanks
    Joel 2:21-27

Lectionary Preaching After Pentecost   53

Introduction

It is a challenging honor to be invited to share these brief sermon manuscripts on the First Lesson texts for the last third of the Sundays after Pentecost in Cycle B.

As I share these brief sermon manuscripts with others, I always find it helpful to remind myself that the sermon manuscript is not the end product of the sermon preparation process. Instead it is only an important and valuable step on the way to the preached sermon. The preached sermon, of course, is what happens in worship during the actual preaching moment. And if the preacher is open to the inspiration of God's Holy Spirit, what happens in the preaching moment cannot be contained within the constraints of any written sermon manuscript!

After reading the assigned texts for these sermons I was challenged by the observation that each of them has a vital message for God's people in their times of trouble. Therefore, the selected title for this book is *When Trouble Comes!* It is shaped by the lessons of life that I have learned from the scriptures and from the "preaching congregations" that have given so much caring and generous feedback to feed me forward in my preaching and teaching ministry. Indeed these congregations have afforded me the opportunity to hear the witness of many "saints" who have been victorious in times of trouble because they have trusted God and relied upon God's promises. Their witness has been a source of strength to me when trouble has come into my life.

Likewise, I hope and pray that these brief sermon manuscripts will help others to experience the truth and power of the words of Jesus when he said: "In the world you face persecution. But take courage; I have conquered the world" (John 16:33).

Zan W. Holmes, Jr.

Job 1:1; 2:1-10

Proper 22
Pentecost 20
Ordinary Time 27

When Trouble Comes!

One of the most realistic stories in the Bible is the story of Job and his troubles.

Job was a good and righteous man whom God blessed abundantly. God blessed him with seven sons and three daughters, a total of ten children, the number which signaled completeness. Likewise, God blessed Job with seven thousand sheep and three thousand camels, again seven plus three, giving us the number of perfection. Furthermore, God blessed Job with five hundred yoke of oxen and five hundred donkeys which also adds up to the perfect number of ten. In other words, the writer of Job wants to make it "perfectly clear" that Job was especially blessed by God. Indeed we are told that Job was the greatest of all the people of the east (1:3). He was so wealthy that each of his sons had an establishment of his own, and they held a family feast each day with the sons taking turns serving as hosts. This too is another sign of blessing for Job. There was harmony in his family. His children all got along with each other.

Furthermore, the biblical text underscores the fact that Job was just as righteous as he was rich and just as good as he was great. In gaining material blessings he did not compromise his soul. In fact, Job was so good and righteous that he had the distinction of having God brag on him! We are told in verse 8 that "the Lord said to Satan, 'Have you considered my servant Job? There is no one like him on earth, a blameless and upright man who fears God and turns away from evil.' "

But one day, like strikes of lightning, four different messengers came to inform Job that trouble had come. One told him his oxen and donkeys had been stolen. The second messenger told him his sheep had been burned up. The third messenger informed him that his camels had been stolen and his servants slain. But the worst was yet to come. A fourth servant arrived and announced the greatest calamity of all. He told Job that each of his seven sons and three daughters had been killed in a hurricane while they were feasting together at the home of the eldest son.

In sum, within a brief period of time, everything that Job had worked for and cherished was lost, and with the exception of his wife, he was left poverty-stricken and alone. So the question arose for Job: What would he do now that trouble had come? Everybody knew what he did when things were going well with him and trouble had not come. But what would he do now that he had received a quadruple dose of trouble?

Well, Job's wife assessed the situation and offered Job a quick way out. She said to him, "Do you still persist in your integrity? Curse God and die."

The Women's Bible Commentary notes: "Job's wife is the one who recognizes, long before Job himself does, what is at stake theologically in innocent suffering: the conflict between innocence and integrity, on the one hand, and an affirmation of the goodness of God on the other."[1]

Job did not follow the advice of his wife, but her words did challenge his thinking. He responded with a question: "Shall we receive the good at the hand of God, and not receive the bad?" (2:10).

Job's question is a question which acknowledges the reality of trouble in his life in spite of his righteousness. He now knew that his righteousness did not necessarily exempt him from trouble. Trouble is an equal opportunity employer. Trouble is a democratic process which does not discriminate against anyone. That is why the title of this sermon is not *"If* Trouble Comes" or "Trouble *Might* Come," but *"When* Trouble Comes." Either we have just come out of a storm or we are in one now. Or one is on the way! Into every life some rain must fall! Jesus never promised us that we would never have trouble. Jesus said: "In this world you face persecution" (John 16:33).

So the issue now for Job was not whether trouble also comes to the righteous. Trouble had already come into his life. The issue for Job was what to do now that trouble had already come. In fact, I believe that *what* happens to us is not as important as how we respond to it.

One response available to Job was the one suggested by his wife. He could have *resigned* and given up his faith in God.

Surely this was one of the response options available to our African American forefathers and foremothers in the face of the troubling contradictions which challenged their faith in the midst of slavery. They observed that many of the people who dealt in the slave traffic were Christians. One of the famous hymn writers, Sir John Newton, made his money from the sale of slaves to the New World. They were troubled by the fact that one famous British slave vessel was named *Jesus*. They were troubled by the fact that the people who bought the slaves were Christians. Likewise, they were troubled by the fact that many Christian ministers, quoting the apostle Paul, gave the sanction of religion to the system of slavery.

Yet in the face of such troubling contradictions, our slave forefathers and foremothers, in their innocent suffering, did not resign and give up their faith in God. To be sure, they had a stubborn faith that enabled them to discern the difference between the God of Christianity and the people who failed to practice it. This discernment is evident in the words of one of the songs they sang: "I've got a robe; you've got a robe. All God's children got a robe. When I get to heaven I'm gonna put on my robe; I'm gonna shout all over God's heaven." And then they looked up at the Big House where the slavemaster lived and they said, "Everybody talking 'bout heaven and going there, heaven, heaven, I'm gonna shout all over God's heaven."

They also sang another song in which they began by saying, "Over my head I see trouble in the air." But then they concluded, "There must be a God somewhere!" Like Job, even though they did not understand their troubles, they refused to resign their faith and let their troubles separate them from God.

Another response option available to Job in the midst of his trouble was the option to *rejoice*. In fact, it is noteworthy to observe the response of Job after he received the bad news reports of the four messengers in chapter one. According to verses 20 and 21, "Job arose, tore his robe, shaved his head, and fell on the ground and worshipped. He said, 'Naked I came from my mother's womb, and naked shall I return there; the Lord gave, and the Lord has taken away; blessed is the name of the Lord.'"

Here Job captures the spirit of the apostle Paul when he said: "Rejoice always, pray without ceasing, give thanks in all circumstances; for this is the will of God in Christ Jesus for you" (1 Thessalonians 5:16-18). Paul did not say give thanks *for* everything. Paul said "*in*" everything give thanks. We can give thanks in trouble because God is with us in trouble to help us accept it and handle it.

Another witness comes to mind. Arthur Ashe, former U.S. champion tennis player, unknowingly and innocently contracted AIDS through a blood transfusion when he underwent a heart-bypass surgery in 1983. At that time hospitals were not checking blood samples for the AIDS virus. He was told he had the virus when he had to have brain surgery in 1988. He had planned to keep the matter a family secret until the news media forced him to confirm or deny the rumor in 1992.

Like Job, Arthur Ashe was faced with the temptation to curse God, resign and give up faith in God. He was tempted to ask, "Why me?" But he said, "If I were to say, 'God, why me?' about the bad things, then I should have said, 'God, why me?' about the good things in life." He said, "Why not me? Why should I be spared what some others have been infected with? And I have to think of all the good of my life, of having a great wife and family and friends and winning Wimbledon and the U.S. Open and playing for and coaching the Davis Cup team, and getting a free scholarship to U.C.L.A. You could also ask about this, 'Why me?' I have always had a religious faith, growing up in the South and having the church as a focal point of my life."[2]

This is the kind of faith that can rejoice and thank God even in the midst of trouble. This is the faith that can worship when trouble comes and celebrate a God who is bigger than any trouble that comes to us.

---

1. *The Women's Bible Commentary*, editors Carol Newsom and Sharon Ringe (Louisville: Westminster/John Knox Press), p. 132.

2. Dennis Kimbro, *Daily Motivations for African Americans* (New York: Fawcett Press), p. 86.

Job 23:1-9, 16-17   Proper 23
                                  Pentecost 21
                              Ordinary Time 28

When We Feel God Has Moved And Left No Forwarding Address

There are times in our lives when we have a greater awareness of God's absence than we do of God's presence. Indeed, this is the experience which confronts Job in our text. In the midst of his suffering he has tried to lay his case before God. He goes forward and backward, to the left and to the right, seeking in every place to find God. To be sure, Job wants to find God because Job knows that he is an innocent sufferer, that he is an upright person. And since God is just, Job is confident that he would gain his acquittal, if only he could gain a hearing before God. But to Job's dismay, God seems to have moved and left no forwarding address. Therefore Job is moved to cry out, "Oh, that I knew where I might find him, that I might come even to his dwelling!" (Job 23:3).

There are many of us who can say "amen" to Job's anguished cry when, in our time of trouble, it seems that God has moved and left no forwarding address. We hear the cry of the troubled Psalmist who said, "My soul thirsts for God, for the living God. When shall I come and behold the face of God? My tears have been my food day and night, while people say to me continually, 'Where is your God?' " (Psalm 42:2-3). We hear the cry of the Hebrew exiles who had trouble finding God in the strange land of Babylon. They said, "By the Rivers of Babylon — there we sat down and there we wept when we remembered Zion. On the willows there we hung our harps. For there our captors asked us for songs, and our tormentors asked for mirth, saying, 'Sing us one of the songs of Zion.' How could we sing the Lord's song in a foreign land?" (Psalm 137:1-4). We hear the cry of the prophet Isaiah who said to God, "Truly, you are a God who hides himself, O God of Israel, the Savior" (Isaiah 45:15). We hear the lonesome cry of the black slaves who sang in their spiritual, "O way down yonder by myself, an' I couldn't hear nobody pray." We even hear the suffering cry of Jesus on the cross when he cried, "My God, my God, why have you forsaken me?" (Mark 15:34). This is scarcely a word which anyone would have invented and put on his lips. This is his own cry, feeling God's absence, identifying with the human cry of feeling oneself shut off from the face of God at the very time when God is needed the most. Indeed if that happened to Jesus himself, then it should not come as a surprise that it happened to one of God's faithful servants like Job or that in spite of our faithfulness there are troubled times when it seems that God has moved and left no forwarding address.

For several months a pastor had been making pastoral calls on a lady who was waging a losing battle against cancer. She was the mother of four small children. She was a faithful Christian, both in the profession of her faith and in the manner by which she lived it. The calm, quiet air of assurance which she always maintained had led many of her friends to declare that she possessed that perfect faith in God which results in simple trust. A few days before her death her pastor stood by her bedside. As he made conversation about ordinary things, a look of eager longing came into her eyes. "Tell me," she pleaded, "where is God now that I need God the most?"

Like Job, she was faced with the challenge of how to remain faithful when it seemed that God had moved and left no forwarding address. To be sure, this is the challenge which faces us in the midst of any crisis in life.

It is a challenge which tempts us to ask: Where is God? What is God doing? Well, God may be giving us the freedom and honor of having a part in determining the final outcome. Or God may be allowing us to experience God's absence so that we can grow and mature in our human responsibility.

One evening when I was leaving a meeting at a church I pastored, I saw one of my members acting very strangely. As he moved along a tree-lined sidewalk he was darting around and behind the trees as if he were hiding from someone. He would pause for a moment behind each tree or bush before quietly moving ahead. When I recognized him, I became curious and concerned, so I called his name. When he heard me calling his name he turned to face me and put his fingers over his lips signaling me to be quiet. He quickly rushed over to me and said, "I know you're wondering why I'm acting so strangely, but I'm following my six-year-old son and I don't want him to see me." He explained that he had allowed his little son to go to the neighborhood store all by himself for the first time. In other words, he was teaching his son to experience the growth that would help him take some initiative in doing something for himself. He had not deserted his son. He was nearby even though his son did not know it. In a loving way this father was giving his son some room for growth.

So sometimes when it appears to us that God has moved and left no forwarding address, it does not mean that God has abandoned us. It may only mean that even though we may not see God, God sees us and God is allowing us room for our faith to grow up. In such times, like Job, we have to keep on seeking God. For faith has been defined in the New Testament as a conviction of a thing not seen.

William Hinson relates the experience of seeing a baby owl in his front lawn as he went out to get the morning paper. He said he did not know what to do about it, so he called a naturalist. The naturalist said, "Don't do anything to that baby owl. If you look up, somewhere in a tall tree you will see he is not alone. His mother has told him to sit very still in order that he might not be seen by a cat or anything else. It takes about two dark nights for a baby owl to spread his wings and fly. In the meantime, if you will look up, you'll see his mother."

William Hinson said he and his wife went out into the yard and looked up into the top of an oak tree and there they saw the mother owl with dark, unblinking eyes fastened on the baby owl and everything and anything that came near him.[1]

When we feel alone and it seems that God has moved out and left no forwarding address, be assured that God knows where we are and God can reach us when God gets ready.

> *Why should I feel discouraged,*
> *Why should the shadows come,*
> *Why should my heart be lonely*
> *and long for heaven and home.*
> *When Jesus is my portion,*
> *my constant friend is He:*
> *His eye is on the sparrow,*
> *And I know He watches me.*[2]

---

1. William Hinson, *A Place to Dig In*, (Abingdon, 1987), pp. 27-28.

2. Charles H. Gabriel, "His Eye Is On the Sparrow," *Songs of Zion*, Supplemental Worship Resources 12, (Abingdon, 1981), p. 33.

Job 38:1-7 (34-41) Proper 24
Pentecost 22
Ordinary Time 29

We Can't Contain God In Our Cups!

One morning a little girl sat at a kitchen table to eat breakfast with her mother and father. As she listened to the prayer her father prayed before the meal, she was especially intrigued that he thanked God for God's presence everywhere.

After the father finished his prayer the little girl asked him, "Father, is it really true that God is everywhere?"

"Yes," said her father.

"Is God in this house?" she asked.

"Yes," her father said.

"Is God in this kitchen?"

"Yes," her father said.

"Is God on this table?" she asked.

"Yes," her father said.

The little girl hesitated and then asked, "Is God in this cup?"

Her father said, "Yes."

Upon hearing this the little girl quickly covered the cup with her hand and exclaimed, "I've got Him!"

In Job's attempt to make some sense out of his suffering, he tried desperately to figure God out by confining God to his own narrow conception of God. In other words, Job was trying to get God to respond within the limited confines of Job's own theological cup. In fact, Job was so certain of his theology that he believed he would prevail if his case were presented before God. To be sure, this is why he wanted to find God. He said, "Would he contend with me in the greatness of his power? No; but he would give heed to me. There an upright person could reason with him, and I should be acquitted forever by my judge" (Job 23:6-7).

Finally in chapter 38 God appears before Job as a voice out of the whirlwind:

> *Who is this that darkens counsel by words without knowledge? Gird up your loins like a man, I will question you, and you shall declare to me. Where were you when I laid the foundation of the earth? Tell me, if you have understanding. Who determined its measurements — surely you know! Or who stretched the line upon it? On what were its bases sunk, or who laid its cornerstone when the morning stars sang together and all the heavenly beings shouted for joy?*
>
> — Job 38:2-7

As soon as God speaks, Job realizes that he can never have the luxury of saying: "I've got God!" Indeed Job now knows that God has exceeded Job's expectations and refuses to be contained and fit neatly into any theological box that Job has constructed.

So God answers Job, but not according to Job's definition of the problem of suffering. Instead God transposes the issue to another level which emphasizes God's power and divine knowledge in contrast to the human weakness and ignorance of Job.[1] In response, Job now realizes how foolish he has been to propose that he understood everything that happens. In fact, Job answers God and says, "See, I am of small account; what shall I answer you? I lay my hand on my mouth.

I have spoken once, and I will not answer; twice, but will proceed no further" (Job 40:4-5).

No longer does Job seek to arrange a debate where he can instruct God. He finally realizes that it is he and not God who is unaware of life's complete picture.

When we too are tempted to believe that God is bound by our theologies, rituals, denominations, and traditions, like Job, we are called to remember that God is boundless and cannot be contained in any of our cups. We cannot put God in the cup of any ritual and say, "I've got God covered." We cannot put God in the cup of any theology and say, "I've got God covered." We cannot put God in the cup of any church tradition and say, "I've got God covered." We cannot put God in any ethnic or gender cup and say, "I've got God covered."

Job learned that God stands above all human systems and wisdom. The purpose behind it all is not to answer directly the problem of suffering, but to give Job a vision of God's glory and presence with Job in the midst of Job's suffering. Thus Job discovers that he can trust God's purposes even though he cannot clearly understand them. Indeed, he comes to see that his new relationship with God will sustain him in the midst of his suffering.

Our African American forefathers and foremothers in the midst of the suffering of slavery could identify with Job's predicament. Even in the face of sorrow and suffering in the absurdity of slavery they were able to sing praises to God through the spirituals. Even though their relationship with God did not bring an immediate end to their oppressive condition, they were sustained by the faith that the cup of slavery could not contain the God of their hope and liberation. By the grace of God, it was a faith that enabled them to sing:

Nobody knows the trouble I see,
Nobody knows but Jesus.
Nobody knows the trouble I see,
Glory, Hallelujah.

---

1. Beverly B. Gaventa, editor, *Texts for Preaching,* (Louisville: Westminster/ John Knox Press, 1993), p. 551.

Job 42:1-6, 10-17   Proper 25
                                    Pentecost 23
                                   Ordinary Time 30

It Came To Pass

One of my father's favorite stories was about a Bible study class that shared their favorite Bible verses with their pastor. When an elderly, uneducated man in the class got his turn to share he said, "Well, I've got a lot of favorite passages that I like a lot, but there's one that has helped me the most. In fact," he said, "it is five little words that are found all over the Bible." When asked what they were, he said: "And it came to pass."

The preacher asked the old man to explain why that was his favorite verse. The old man said, "Don't you see? When the Bible says, 'It came to pass,' that means that it did not come to stay." He said, "During my life many troubles have come, but thank God, they did not come to stay. Instead, they came to pass."

I believe that Job could say "amen" to this old man's favorite Bible passage. In the first chapter of the Book of Job we are given a graphic description of the troubles that came into Job's life. In quick succession on the very same day, a series of messengers came to inform him of the trouble that had come. One told him that all of his oxen and donkeys had been stolen and his servants slain. Another messenger arrived to tell him that his sheep and the servants who cared for them had been destroyed by fire. A third then appeared and informed him that all his camels had been stolen and the servants who cared for them slain. Finally, a fourth servant came and told Job that his sons and daughters had been killed in a storm. And, to add insult to injury, we are told in chapter two of the Book of Job that Job was infected with sores from the sole of his foot to the crown of his head.

Without a doubt, Job was indeed a troubled man. To be sure, Job's troubles were compounded by the fact that he believed he did not deserve them. Indeed, he considered himself a righteous and blameless man.

However, after 41 chapters in which Job engages his wife, friends, and God in self-righteous debate about the fairness of his troubled life, resolution finally comes to him in chapter 42. Here we discover the truth of the old man's favorite Bible verse in the life of Job. Job's troubles did not come to stay. Instead, they came to pass. To be sure, we are told that "the Lord restored the fortunes of Job when he had prayed for his friends; and the Lord gave Job twice as much as he had before" (Job 42:10).

Walter Brueggeman and James Newsome warn us that it is tempting to read verses 10-17 as an effort to connect divine rewards to human righteousness since Job repents (v. 6) and God restored his fortunes fourfold. However, this would contradict the basic message of the book. Furthermore, Job was blameless and upright when God first permitted Satan to torment Job. Therefore, Brueggeman and Newsome suggest that the restoration of Job's fortunes should be read as an expression not of God's justice, but of God's mercy.[1] Indeed, since Job had repented of his arrogance before God, his faith did not depend upon divine rewards anymore.

Nevertheless, Job's story is still a testimony to the fact that, by the grace of God, his troubles did not come to stay, but came to pass. Indeed, it is a reminder that when we are in trouble, God cares about us and is actually involved to deliver us and restore us.

This is the witness of the apostle Paul when he says "We know that all things work together for good for those who love God, who are called according to his purpose" (Romans 8:28). This does not mean that all things automatically work together for good in every situation for everybody. It means that all things work together for good for those who *love* God! Because to love God is to cooperate with God in our times of trouble.

Job suffered with God but repented and ended up cooperating with God's plan to start Job's life over. After all the suffering and grief he experienced, Job could have been gun-shy about doing it all again. He could have resigned and retired. He could have become resentful and bitter. But instead he had the love and trust to cooperate with God and start it all over again.

It is not easy for any of us to cooperate with God and do it all over again when we have experienced the pain of trouble; when we have experienced the pain of divorce; when we have experienced the pain of physical, sexual, and mental abuse; when we have experienced the pain of betrayal; when we have experienced the pain of personal and institutional failure; when we have experienced the pain of an injury or illness; when we have experienced the pain of racism and sexism; when we have experienced the pain of a pregnancy out of wedlock; when we have experienced the pain of self-righteousness. So even though our troubles do not come to stay but come to pass, our greatest challenge is to cooperate with God's plan to restore us by starting all over again.

When, like Job, we have the trust and love to cooperate with God, God will work all things together for good.

This is the message of the African saying that "you can't tell how bread tastes by tasting the individual ingredients." Instead, we have to wait until all the ingredients have been worked together to see how the bread tastes. No wonder the psalmist said, "O taste and see that the Lord is good" (Psalm 34:8).

As Job's troubles came to pass, we are told: "Then there came to him ... all who had known him before, and they ate bread with him in his house; they showed him sympathy and comforted him for all the evil that the Lord had brought upon him; and each of them gave him a piece of money and a gold ring. The Lord blessed the latter days of Job more than his beginning ..." (Job 42:11-12).

Let us rejoice that our troubles do not last always. By the grace of God we shall overcome!

---

1. Beverly B. Gaventa, editor, *Texts For Preaching,* (Louisville: Westminster/ John Knox Press, 1993).

Ruth 1:1-18

Proper 26
Pentecost 24
Ordinary Time 31

From Singleness To Solidarity

The book of Ruth is one of the world's most beautiful stories of human solidarity in the face of trouble.

Apart from the book of Esther it is the only other book in the Bible to be named after a woman. Therefore it should not be a surprise that the major characters of the book are two women, Naomi and Ruth. A major theme of the book is their common struggle to survive in the midst of a hostile and troubled environment.

The stage was set for their common struggle when a food famine occurred in the city of Bethlehem. This was somewhat of a paradoxical event, for the word "Bethlehem" means "house of bread" in the Hebrew language. Surely, of all places, no one expected a food shortage to occur in the "house of bread." Nevertheless, the famine in Bethlehem is a reminder that no place or person is exempt from trouble. Into every life some rain will fall.

As a result of the food crisis in Bethlehem, Elimelech took his wife Naomi and their two sons, Mahlon and Chilion, and moved into the country of Moab and settled there (Ruth 1:1-2). They evidently thought that they would fare better there. But they soon learned that they could not run away from trouble. Shortly after they arrived in Moab, Elimelech died, and Naomi was left as a single parent with two sons in a foreign land.

Nevertheless, Naomi and her two sons remained in the foreign land of Moab. Even though they were Hebrews, each of her sons married a foreign wife from Moab. One of the wives was Orpah, which means in Hebrew "she who turns back." The other was named Ruth, which in Hebrew means "companion."

But Naomi's two sons, Mahlon and Chilion, were not very healthy men, as indicated by their names. In fact, Hebrew names were not selected before a child was born, but at birth. Then they often reflected some of the circumstances surrounding the condition of the child at birth. In Hebrew "Mahlon" means "sickly one" and Chilion means "wasting away." So after ten short years of marriage it is no surprise that Mahlon and Chilion both died and left their wives, Orpah and Ruth, without children.

Now the story presents us with three single women who are trying to survive in a time of trouble. Therefore, one of the questions raised by this biblical story is: "How do single women survive in a time of trouble?"

Furthermore, their singleness was complicated and compounded by several other factors. Not only were they single women, but also they were single, *widowed* women. Not only were they single, widowed women, but also they were single, widowed women who *had no children*, especially male heirs who were prized during that time. Not only were they single, widowed women who had no children, but also they were *poor,* single, widowed women without children. Furthermore, they were not only poor, widowed, single women without children, but they were living in a male dominated culture in which women had no rights and were both the property and responsibility of men. To be sure, they are representative of all the socially, economically, politically, and spiritually oppressed women of their day and time, as well as ours.

They represent all single women who have been wounded and rejected by the tragic circumstances of life. They represent all single women who have lost loved ones by death, divorce, or separation and feel they have to face the future alone. They represent all single women who are single not by choice but by circumstances. They represent all people who stand on the brink of some uncertain future.

So what are these three single women going to do in the midst of their troubled situation? Well, note that before they do anything they are greeted by a gracious word from the Lord. Naomi heard that the Lord had considered his people and had given them food (verse 6). We are not told how she heard about it. But somehow, even though she was in a foreign land, she must have kept in touch with her people back home in Bethlehem. This is a reminder to us that God has a liberating word for us in every situation. However, it is our responsibility to hear that word and respond to it by cooperating with God.

In response to the word that she had heard from God, Naomi cooperated by making the decision to return home alone to Bethlehem. As a matter of fact, she suggested to Orpah and Ruth that perhaps the best way for them to deal with their common crisis was for all three of them to go their separate ways.

Orpah agreed. Indeed, she was bound by her name, which means in Hebrew "she who turns back." So she departed to bear her singleness all alone and was never to be heard from again.

But Ruth made the decision to bear her singleness in solidarity with the singleness of Naomi. In one of the most beautiful statements of human solidarity in the Bible, she says to Naomi:

> *Do not press me to leave you*
> *or to turn back from following you!*
> *Where you go, I will go;*
> *Where you lodge, I will lodge;*
> *your people shall be my people,*
> *and your God my God.*
> *Where you die, I will die —*
> *there will I be buried.*
> *May the Lord do thus and so to me,*
> *and more as well,*
> *if even death parts me from you!*
>
> — vv. 16-17

So Naomi and Ruth returned to Bethlehem together. In response to the word of God that food was available in Bethlehem, they organized their singleness. Instead of saying "to each her own," they pooled their resources and got them all together in the name of God. Thus, they became one of the first single women's support groups in the Bible. Hand in hand, over the hills and mountains, and down through the valleys, they eventually made it back to Bethlehem and overcame the threat of famine. By the grace of God they were sustained on their journey because they shared their singleness in solidarity with God and each other.

A familiar African fable tells about a group of people on earth who wanted to know the difference between heaven and hell. A tour was arranged so they could see for themselves. In hell they saw all of the people sitting across from each other at long tables. There was plenty of food on the tables. However the people in hell were starving and frail because their arms were taped with splints so that they could not bend their elbows and get the food from the tables to their mouths.

When the people on the tour arrived in heaven they were surprised to see some of the same conditions. The people in heaven also sat at long tables across from each other. They also had their arms taped with splints so that they could not bend their elbows to get food from the tables to their mouths. However, there were two major differences. First, the people in heaven were healthy and well fed. Second, they were healthy and well fed because each person overcame the problem of not being able to feed himself by picking up food and feeding the person across the table. Like Naomi and Ruth, their decision to share their singleness in solidarity saved them from starvation.

By the grace of God:
If there is a problem, we can solve it together!
If there is a burden, we can lift it together!
If there is a mountain, we can climb it together!
If there is a stone, we can move it together!
If there is a challenge, we can meet it together!
If there is a race, we can run it together!
If there is a river, we can cross it together!

Isaiah 25:6-9   All Saints' Sunday

Guess Who's Coming To Dinner?

In 1967 Stanley Kramer produced and directed the Oscar-winning movie *Guess Who's Coming to Dinner?* Two of the stars of the movie were a young black man, portrayed by Sidney Poitier, and his fiancée, a young white woman who was portrayed by Katherine Houghton.

The suspense of the movie revolves around the decision of Katherine to invite Sidney to a dinner in the home of her white parents without informing them that Sidney is black. So since this was an unlikely happening in many places in America, even as late as 1967, the movie was titled *Guess Who's Coming to Dinner?* Indeed it was a movie that dared to lift for us a vision of inclusion in a society known for its practice of exclusion.

Likewise, our text lifts up a similar vision of inclusion for another society known for its exclusion. In fact, Isaiah 25:6-9 lifts up the vision of a radical transformation of the human situation of exclusion. Like the movie, its main image is a meal. Indeed, it is a banquet that the Lord will prepare on Mount Zion in which "all peoples" are invited to participate (v. 6). It is also an occasion that will inaugurate a new age of joy and peace in which God will "swallow up death forever" and will "wipe away the tears from all faces" (vv. 7-8). Thus it is an eschatological banquet that will usher in the reign of God on behalf of a new Israel consisting of all peoples.

I was reminded of the challenge of this vision for our own time as I participated in a family banquet gathering during one Thanksgiving season. After the meal I pulled out my camera and began to take pictures of various family members. When I got to my last frame I announced that I wanted everybody to gather for a picture of our whole family. Upon hearing my announcement, the eyes of my little eight-year-old nephew lit up. He immediately rushed out the door into the front yard and shouted to his friends in the neighborhood, "Hey, everybody, come on!" Of course, this presented a very awkward moment for me. I had to explain what I meant when I used the term "everybody." I was using "everybody" in an exclusive manner. I was including everybody in our immediate family who was gathered in the house. Thus, I was excluding everybody else in the neighborhood and community. I confess that my explanation was puzzling and confusing to my eight-year-old nephew. In fact, I was challenged by his vision of "everybody" because it was far closer to Isaiah's vision than mine.

So our text today challenges all of our limited visions of family, race, church, community, denomination, nation, culture, and neighborhood, which exclude others from our understanding of who "everybody" is. We are reminded that "God so loved the *world* that he gave his only Son, so that *everyone* who believes in him may not perish, but have eternal life" (John 3:16).

Our text is one of the selected readings for the celebration of All Saints. It inspires us to remember and thank God for "all saints" who have given their lives that all of God's people might be invited to a banquet that will transform a world known for its exclusion.

One "saint" who comes to mind is congressman Mickey Leland. He died in a plane crash on August 7, 1989, while he was on a famine-relief mission in Africa. As chairperson of the House Select Committee on Hunger he visited Ethiopia and Sudan at least six times in six years. His access to the so-called Third World continued and even Marxist leaders allowed him to help free political prisoners in Cuba, a jailed American aviator in Angola, and children who wanted to leave Vietnam to be with relatives in America.

When he was criticized by some for spending time away from his home country and home district, he replied by saying, "I am as much a citizen of this world as I am of this country … I grew up on a Christian ethic which says we are supposed to help the least of our brothers and sisters. We are only a reflection of the people we are called to serve." Because he was a servant-leader for the world neighborhood, he captured Isaiah's vision and thereby enabled people to cross dividing lines and rally together around the commitment to provide bread for "all peoples." Therefore it was no mere coincidence that among those who died with him in his final mission on behalf of the "least of these" were African Americans, whites, seven Ethiopians, Christians, and Ivan Tilliem, a Jewish philanthropist and anti-hunger advocate. So Mickey died as he lived, a citizen of the world. So likewise our text calls us to live, serve, and die, knowing that God wants everybody to come to dinner at the Lord's table. We also know that this is the same God who "swallows up death forever . . . and wipes away the tears from all faces" (Isaiah 25:7-8). Hallelujah and praise God!

Ruth 3:1-5; 4:13-17

Proper 27
Pentecost 25
Ordinary Time 32

From Rejection To Redemption

Gloria Steinem has written a book titled *Marilyn*. It is based on the life of Marilyn Monroe, the Hollywood movie queen of the 1950s who lived an up and down life and eventually ended her life by committing suicide.

In the book Gloria Steinem tells of a brief conversation that Marilyn Monroe had with her maid toward the end of her life. Marilyn said, "Nobody's ever gonna love me now, Lena. What good am I? I can't have kids. I can't cook. I've been divorced three times. Who would want me?" Her maid Lena said: "Why, millions of men would want you!" Marilyn said: "Yeah, Lena, millions of men would want me, but who would really love me?"

I imagine that there is a sense in which Naomi and Ruth in our biblical text could identify with Marilyn Monroe. They too had experienced some ups and downs in their lives. They also had experienced the feeling of rejection which was often directed toward poor, single, and widowed women who had come upon hard times in the male-dominated culture of their day. They, too, had probably wondered what man would really love them after all they had been through.

But Naomi and Ruth did not sink beneath the weight of their difficult circumstances. Instead they prevailed over their circumstances because they had two things going for them.

First, Naomi and Ruth had their common loyalty and support for each other going for them. As we noted in the previous sermon, they responded to their difficult circumstances by sharing their common singleness in a common act of solidarity and mutual support.

In fact, it was the loyalty and support that Ruth gave to Naomi that eventually won for Ruth the notice of Boaz, who was Naomi's kinsman on her husband's side. Ruth had gone to work as a gleaner in the fields of Boaz. Thereupon she gained favor with Boaz, who told her to remain in his fields close to the reapers. Furthermore, he offered her protection from the young men.

When Ruth asked why she had found such special favor from Boaz, he said: "All that you have done for your mother-in-law since the death of your husband has been fully told me, and how you left your father and mother and your native land and came to a people that you did not know before. May the Lord reward you for your deeds, and may you have a full reward from the Lord, the God of Israel, under whose wings you have come for refuge" (Ruth 2:11-12).

Indeed Boaz was not only impressed by Ruth's loyalty to Naomi, he was also eventually impressed by her loyalty to him in spite of the fact that she had the opportunity to go after the men who were younger than he (3:10). So he eventually offered Ruth the gifts of marriage and security by acting as her next of kin. In fact, the proposal of Boaz to act as Ruth's next of kin is a further reflection of the solidarity and relationship of Ruth and Naomi. Boaz was a kinsman of Naomi's husband, but Naomi had enlarged her family to include Ruth. She had already said to Ruth, "The man (Boaz) is a relative of *ours*, one of our nearest kin" (2:20). Thus, Boaz is not just Naomi's relative, he is Ruth's as well.

This is significant for our story. In the culture of Israel, the kinsman was not just a relative. A kinsman was someone bound by custom to take the side of those who were in trouble. Indeed the term *kinsman* was also used to mean *redeemer*. If trouble came to one family member, it became the responsibility of the next of kin to redeem the situation.

In fact, Naomi and Ruth had apparently forgotten that there was an unnamed kinsman who had the first right of refusal to the heritage of Elimelech which would have allowed him to claim Ruth as his wife. However, he allowed his obligation to pass to Boaz (4:6) and Boaz said to the elder and all the people: "Today you are witnesses that I have acquired from the hand of Naomi all that belonged to Elimelech and all that belonged to Chilion and Mahlon. I have also acquired Ruth the Moabite the wife of Mahlon, to be my wife . . ." (4:9-10).

Thus Boaz and Ruth married. They bore a son. Naomi became the child's nurse. The child, Obed, became the grandfather of none other than King David. Ruth and Naomi had indeed moved all the way from rejection to redemption; a story that began with trouble ends with the birth of a child.

But it was not only because they had their common loyalty and solidarity going for them. Above all, they also had God going for them. It is more than a story of human solidarity, perseverance, and romance. It is also the story of how God works in the midst of troubled circumstances to bring hope and redemption. To be sure it is an expression of the African-American church tradition that "the Lord can make a way out of no way!"

Another witness comes to mind. Mary McCloud Bethune was born on a farm July 10, 1875, near Mayesville, South Carolina. She was the fifteenth child of former slaves, yet she acquired a passion for education that would help redeem the lives of poor and oppressed blacks. In 1904 she moved to Daytona Beach, Florida, and took $1.50 and opened a school, which at its inception had four little black girls and her son as its student body. Her husband eventually left for another town and died after a few years. But even though she was a poor, single woman in a racially oppressive society, she kept her dream alive. She baked sweet potato pies and sold them to railroad construction crews. She went from door to door asking for contributions of money or goods. She eventually attracted the interest and support of James M. Gamble, the soap manufacturer. Local blacks and whites also caught her vision and joined in solidarity with her. By 1907 she was able to raise enough funds to see the first actual building for her school constructed. She appropriately named it Faith Hall! Today because of the faith of Mary McCloud Bethune, Bethune-Cookman College in Daytona Beach, Florida, is a vital and thriving United Methodist Church related college still committed to a faith that God can "make a way out of no way" and bring redemption to the rejected.

Let the redeemed of the Lord say so! (Psalm 107:2).

1 Samuel 1:4-20　　　　　　　　　　Proper 28
　　　　　　　　　　　　　　　　　Pentecost 26
　　　　　　　　　　　　　　　　Ordinary Time 33

When The Odds Are Against Us

I recently had the privilege of introducing Maya Angelou who addressed a luncheon honoring Cecil Williams at Perkins School of Theology. Ms. Angelou, a world renowned poet, writer, and actress, is author of the best-selling book *I Know Why the Caged Bird Sings* and is perhaps best remembered for her poem, "On the Pulse of the Morning," which she read at the inauguration of President William Jefferson Clinton on January 20, 1993.

As I listened to her eloquent and challenging address, I was especially inspired when I recalled how God had given her the grace to overcome the great odds against her.

For example, I remembered that as a result of being sexually abused by her mother's boyfriend, she was a mute for five years of her childhood. She was further abused by others who called her a moron and an idiot. But she said that her grandmother told her all the time, "Sister, Mama don't care what these people say about you being a moron, being an idiot. Mama don't care. Mama know sister, when you and the good Lord get ready, you're going to be a preacher."[1] These words of her grandmother helped Maya Angelou to overcome the odds against her.

Like Maya Angelou, Hannah in our text was confronted with some great odds that were against her. Hannah was one of two wives of Elkanah. Peninnah, the other wife, had several sons and daughters. However, Hannah had no children because God had "closed her womb." This was indeed a situation of great odds against Hannah because in her day a woman's primary role was to bear children. It was the means by which a woman's status and worth were measured. Therefore, barrenness was a mark of disgrace.

The odds against Hannah were compounded by the fact that Peninnah made Hannah's life miserable by ridiculing and taunting her because of the differences in their families. Likewise, the well-intentioned pity of Elkanah further compounded the odds against Hannah. He tried to console her but he did not understand the depth of her unhappiness. Although she was his favorite wife in spite of her barrenness, that did not satisfy her need to have children for her own personal fulfillment. In addition, the odds against Hannah were stacked high because, unlike Maya Angelou, she had no grandmother or any other family member who gave her words of encouragement.

But in spite of the great odds against her, Hannah reached down within herself and did an amazing thing. We are told that "Hannah rose and presented herself to the Lord" (v. 9). In other words, she refused to let the odds against her get her down or keep her down! She *rose* up and went to the temple at Shiloh to present her case before the Lord in prayer.

She reminds me of my African American slave foremothers and forefathers who always found comfort and strength in worship when the odds were so greatly against them. They too were ridiculed and taunted and called everything but a child of God. But they did not derive their identity from the names their slavemasters called them. Instead, like Hannah, they *rose* and presented themselves before the Lord. To be sure, they stole away and they sang a song: "Hush, hush, Somebody's calling my name." And then they sang another verse: "It sounds like Jesus, Somebody's calling my name." This was a major resource that empowered them to overcome the odds against them, and it is our most major resource today.

Hannah prayed to the Lord and made a vow. She said, "O Lord of hosts, if only you will look on the misery of your servant, and remember me, and not forget your servant, but will give to your servant a male child, then I will set him before you as a nazirite until the day of his death ..." (v. 11).

However as Hannah continued to pray she had to overcome the odds that were stacked against her in the temple worship. Maybe she got too emotional for the staid worship to which the priest Eli was accustomed in the temple. Maybe she became so filled with God's spirit that she shook her body too much for Eli. Maybe Eli thought she was praying so long that the service might go beyond one hour! Maybe she was not following the prescribed ritual! Whatever the reason, Eli the priest thought that she was drunk with wine and chastised her. He said to her, "How long will you make a drunken spectacle of yourself? Put away your wine!" (v. 14). In other words he was telling her, "You are out of order!"

Sometimes in the church today we fail to minister to those who have great odds stacked against them because we fail to look beyond our prejudices and rituals and see their real need.

Bishop Noah Moore, Jr., often told of a woman who came to the altar during one of the worship services when he pastored the Tindley Temple United Methodist Church in Philadelphia, Pennsylvania. He said that the woman's clothes were torn. Her hair was not combed and her eyes were red and bloodshot. Assuming her to be drunk with alcohol, he said to her: "Daughter, you know better than to come to church drunk like this."

She said, "Pastor, please let me pray. You don't understand. I had to fight my husband in order to get out of the house to come to church and I will have to fight to get back in. But I had to come here this morning to get the strength to make it another week."

We never know what people are going through when they come to worship. Thank God that Hannah did not accept Eli's misreading of her situation without speaking up and voicing her concern. And thank God that Eli accepted her response. He said to her: "Go in peace; the God of Israel grant the petition you have made to him" (v. 17). With those words of benediction the story reaches its God-given conclusion. In spite of the odds against her, by the grace of God Hannah will bear her son.

After her son Samuel is born Hannah keeps her vow to the Lord. She says: "For this child I prayed; and the Lord has granted me the petition that I made to him. Therefore I have lent him to the Lord; as long as he lives, he is given to the Lord" (vv. 27-28).

If Hannah had not risen up and turned to the Lord she would not have overcome the great odds against her, and neither will we. This is the same God who told Abraham and Sarah that they would have a child in their old age. This is the same God who called Noah to build an ark, even when no rain was in sight. This is the same God who told Joshua the walls of Jericho would fall if he led the children of Israel around it seven times. All of this was against great odds. But Isaac was born. The rain did come. The wall did fall. And Samuel was born to Hannah and Elkanah. Hallelujah! God is able!

---

1. Maya Angelou, *I Dream A World, Portraits of Black Women*, p. 68.

2 Samuel 23:1-7   Christ The King

From The Redemption Of A King To A King Of Redemption

A visitor once entered a large cathedral to spend some time in meditation. As he reflected upon the sins of his own life, he looked up and saw statues of biblical saints that had been placed in great niches along the high walls of the cathedral. Included among them were Moses, David, and Peter. Suddenly he remembered that each one of them was also a person who had sinned and made mistakes in life. But by the grace of God they had been redeemed and were now counted among the saints in the Bible.

To be sure on Christ the King Sunday, our text (2 Samuel 23:1-7) deals with the last words of a king who was redeemed by the grace of God. We remember the occasion of his most notable sin and failure: one evening as he walked around the walls of his palace he saw Bathsheba bathing and sent for her. Although she was the wife of another man, King David slept with her. In order to conceal his deed, he had her husband, Uriah, placed in the forefront of an upcoming battle — then had his general order the rest of the army to fall back so Uriah would be killed. King David them claimed Bathsheba for himself.

But what made David's sin so great and notable is that David was the king! Uriah was his subject. David represented the host country. Uriah was the Hittite, the stranger, an alien who had married into the tribe. David, the king, represented the powerful. Uriah represented the powerless.

However, David the King was soon to discover that God stands on the side of justice. God sent Nathan, a country preacher, to convict the king of his sin. Nathan simply told David this story:

"There were two men in certain city, the one rich and the other poor. The rich man had very many flocks and herds; but the poor man had nothing but one little ewe lamb ... Now there came a traveler to the rich man, and he was loathe to take one of his own flock or herd to prepare for the wayfarer who had come to him, but he took the poor man's lamb, and prepared that for the guest who had come to him" (2 Samuel 12:1-4).

When David heard the story he angrily demanded to know what man had done such a thing. Whereupon Nathan said to the king, "You are the man" (v. 7).

But as we remember the occasion of King David's most notable sin and conviction, we also remember the occasion of his compassion, repentance, and redemption! In response to his conviction, he did not have Nathan beheaded. Nor did he order a cover-up. Instead he fell on his knees and cried out to God, his redeemer: "Have mercy on me, O God, according to your steadfast love; according to your abundant mercy, blot out my transgressions. Wash me thoroughly from my iniquity, and cleanse me from my sin ... Against you, you alone, have I sinned, and done what is evil in your sight ... Create in me a clean heart, O God, and put a new and right spirit within me ... Restore to me the joy of your salvation, and sustain in me a willing spirit. Then will I teach transgressors your ways, and sinners will return to you" (Psalm 51:1-2, 4a, 10, 12-13).

So, in 2 Samuel 23:1-7 we see the fruits of a redeemed king. In his last words he affirms that it is the "spirit of the Lord" that speaks through him (v. 2). In this last will and testament he affirms his commitment to a being who rules with justice and in the fear of the Lord (v. 3). Then he leaves to his successors an "everlasting covenant" made by God (v. 5). In other words, at the heart of the theology of the Davidic Covenant was the understanding that the individual who sat on Jerusalem's throne would ensure the well-being of all individuals within the kingdom.[1] By the grace of God, this is the leadership symbolized in David, the redeemed king.

On this Christ the King Sunday, David the redeemed king is also a symbol of hope for us all. It is a symbol of hope for the man who sat in the large cathedral and reflected on his sins. It is a symbol of hope for all who know failure. Redemption is available in every situation. In fact, the good news for us is that we have a king of redemption in Jesus Christ. To be sure, Jesus is a descendant of David, was born in David's home town, Bethlehem, and many call him the Son of David. So that our history of redemption journeys from a redeemed King David to the King of Redemption who is Jesus Christ the Son of David. The grace of God is indeed an awesome thing.

I once heard the story of a dilapidated little shop whose owner was about to go out of business. The floor was unswept, the windows unwashed, the goods in disorder, and the proprietor careless and untidy. One day the king came by, saw the wretched condition of the place, and said to the shopkeeper, "If you will do as I say, I will let you put over the door 'approved by the king.'" The proprietor gladly consented. Everything was changed; the floor was swept, the windows washed, the goods in order, and the keeper himself cleaned up.

Soon customers began to come and money rang in the cash register because of the approval of the king. Hallelujah! Have you ever let the king take over your life? Have we ever said: "Into my heart, into my heart, come into my heart, Lord Jesus. Come in today. Come in to stay. Come into my heart, Lord Jesus."

---

1. Beverly B. Gaventa, editor, *Texts for Preaching*, (Louisville: Westminster/ John Knox Press, 1993), p. 597.

Joel 2:21-27　　　　　　　　　　Thanksgiving Day

When It's Hard To Give Thanks

Henry Ossawa Tanner (1859-1937) was the first black artist to acquire an international reputation in this century. He remains well known today in museum and academic circles, although his name is not familiar to a more general audience.

One of his most popular paintings is titled *The Thankful Poor*. It is a painting which features an elderly father and his little son as they are seated at a table to eat a meal. There is no fancy turkey with dressing. There is no cranberry sauce. There are no sweet potatoes. There is no pumpkin pie. Instead there is only one tiny dish of food for them to share.

But yet, in spite of their limited resources, their heads are bowed in prayer to give thanks to God for what little they have. Although they are poor, they are thankful to God.

On the other hand, that is not always an easy thing to do. There are times when it is hard to give thanks in the midst of life's inequities. When bad things happen to good people it is not always so easy to give thanks. Sometimes when things are not going our way, it is hard to give thanks. When trouble comes, we sometimes find it easier to complain to God rather than give thanks for what we have.

In fact, this is the experience of the people of Judah in the book of Joel. They were faced with a major disaster. Their crops were being destroyed by a plague of swarming locusts. This was especially tragic for them because they were an agricultural community which depended upon the produce of their crops to sustain them physically, socially, and economically. Furthermore the spiritual life of the people was impacted by the plague. Because their animals died from lack of food, they had none left to sacrifice in the temple, a ritual which had been performed as an offering to God without cessation for centuries. This, of course, was a thing that distressed Joel the priest deeply. In fact the temple worship had become so dependent upon animal sacrifice that the people found it difficult to praise God in other ways. It was hard for them to give thanks.

Therefore, instead of giving thanks, the people began to complain to God. Faith shifted to fatalism. Courage changed to cynicism. Hope went on a holiday. There was no faith to be fired, no prayer to be prayed and no song to be sung. And so they were about to give up on their future because of a setback that they had suffered.

Have you ever been there? Chances are that at some time in our lives, each of us has suffered a serious setback. It may be a financial or career setback. It may be a physical or spiritual setback. It may be a social or mental setback. Churches are not exempt from setbacks. Families are not exempt. Nations and communities are not exempt. Jesus never promised us that we would not have tribulations. And in such times our faith in God is challenged and we, too, like Judah find it hard to give thanks to God.

But during this season of Thanksgiving, Joel has a twofold word for all who find it hard to give thanks in the midst of trouble. First, he called the people of Judah to repentance and prayer. He said, "Sanctify a fast, call a solemn assembly.

Gather the elders and all the inhabitants of the land to the house of the Lord your God, and cry out to the Lord" (1:14). Joel also told them to "rend your hearts and not your clothing. Return to the Lord your God, for he is gracious and merciful, slow to anger, and abounding in steadfast love, and relents from punishing" (Joel 2:12-13).

Upon their return to the Lord they were able to get a meaningful perspective upon their crisis. They were like the man who took his first trip to New York. He visited the Empire State Building, which at the time was the tallest building in the world. He stood on the same side of the street on which the building was located and strained his back as he leaned back and tried to see the top of the building. A nearby guide saw him and said, "Sir, you are too close to the building to see it. You have to move back from it in order to get a full view of it."

After their repentance and return to the Lord, the people were able to see that more was going on in the midst of their crisis than they could originally see. They now saw that God was using their crisis to bring them to their senses. God was seeking to prepare them for the Day of the Lord which was an even greater challenge than the plague of locusts. It is a reminder that God does not bring us through the waters to drown us, but to save us. And God does not bring us through the fire to burn us, but to purify us.

This does not mean that God sends every crisis which comes into our lives. We often bring our setbacks upon ourselves. But it does mean that God can use our setbacks as a set up for a comeback! In fact, God heard the cry of the people and brought them back by reversing their bad fortune. God promised them that they would have "abundant rain" (v. 23) and that "the threshing floors shall be full of grain, and the vats shall overflow with wine and oil" (v. 24). Further, the

Lord said, "I will repay you for the years that the swarming locust has eaten ..." (v. 25).

The people learned that there are countless reasons to give thanks, even in the midst of trouble, because through it all God is at work to save us.

A pastor known for his pulpit prayers always found something to thank God for, even in troubled times. On one dark stormy day when he had experienced some personal tragedy in his own life, his members said: "Surely the Pastor will have nothing to thank God for on a morning like this."

But as the preacher began his prayer, he said: "Lord, we know that this is a dreary morning. But, Lord, let us learn from our troubles and be reminded that it has not always been like this. You have given us days of sunshine. And we have enough faith to thank you ahead of time that it will not always be like this in the future. By your grace we believe that there is a bright side somewhere and the sun will shine again. We believe that new life is possible and you have the future in your hand. We believe your grace has brought us safe thus far, and we believe your grace will lead us home."

Trouble does come. But Jesus always comes to help us meet it and overcome it. During this Thanksgiving season let us give thanks that there is power in his purpose, joy in his justice, glory in his grace, and deliverance in his deeds. Let the church say, Amen!

Lectionary Preaching After Pentecost

The following index will aid the user of this book in matching the correct text to the correct Sunday with the appropriate text during Pentecost. All texts in this book are from the series for Lesson One, Revised Common Lectionary. (*Note that the ELCA division of Lutheranism is now following the Revised Common Lectionary.*) The Lutheran and Roman Catholic designations indicate days comparable to Sundays on which Revised Common Lectionary Propers are used.

(Fixed dates do not pertain to Lutheran Lectionary)

Fixed Date Lectionaries *Revised Common (including ELCA)* *and Roman Catholic*	**Lutheran Lectionary** *Lutheran*
The Day of Pentecost	The Day of Pentecost
The Holy Trinity	The Holy Trinity
May 29-June 4 — Proper 4, Ordinary Time 9	Pentecost 2
June 5-11 — Proper 5, Ordinary Time 10	Pentecost 3
June 12-18 — Proper 6, Ordinary Time 11	Pentecost 4
June 19-25 — Proper 7, Ordinary Time 12	Pentecost 5
June 26-July 2 — Proper 8, Ordinary Time 13	Pentecost 6
July 3-9 — Proper 9, Ordinary Time 14	Pentecost 7
July 10-16 — Proper 10, Ordinary Time 15	Pentecost 8
July 17-23 — Proper 11, Ordinary Time 16	Pentecost 9
July 24-30 — Proper 12, Ordinary Time 17	Pentecost 10
July 31-Aug. 6 — Proper 13, Ordinary Time 18	Pentecost 11
Aug. 7-13 — Proper 14, Ordinary Time 19	Pentecost 12
Aug. 14-20 — Proper 15, Ordinary Time 20	Pentecost 13
Aug. 21-27 — Proper 16, Ordinary Time 21	Pentecost 14
Aug. 28-Sept. 3 — Proper 17, Ordinary Time 22	Pentecost 15
Sept. 4-10 — Proper 18, Ordinary Time 23	Pentecost 16

Sept. 11-17 — Proper 19, Ordinary Time 24	Pentecost 17
Sept. 18-24 — Proper 20, Ordinary Time 25	Pentecost 18
Sept. 25-Oct. 1 — Proper 21, Ordinary Time 26	Pentecost 19
Oct. 2-8 — Proper 22, Ordinary Time 27	Pentecost 20
Oct. 9-15 — Proper 23, Ordinary Time 28	Pentecost 21
Oct. 16-22 — Proper 24, Ordinary Time 29	Pentecost 22
Oct. 23-29 — Proper 25, Ordinary Time 30	Pentecost 23
Oct. 30-Nov. 5 — Proper 26, Ordinary Time 31	Pentecost 24
Nov. 6-12 — Proper 27, Ordinary Time 32	Pentecost 25
Nov. 13-19 — Proper 28, Ordinary Time 33	Pentecost 26
	Pentecost 27
Nov. 20-26 — Christ the King	Christ the King

Reformation Day (or last Sunday in October) is October 31 (Revised Common, Lutheran)

All Saints' Day (or first Sunday in November) is November 1 (Revised Common, Lutheran, Roman Catholic)

Books In This Cycle B Series

Gospel Set

God's Downward Mobility
Sermons For Advent, Christmas And Epiphany
John A. Stroman

Which Way To Jesus?
Sermons For Lent And Easter
Harry N. Huxhold

Water Won't Quench The Fire
Sermons For Pentecost (First Third)
William G. Carter

Fringe, Front And Center
Sermons For Pentecost (Middle Third)
George W. Hoyer

No Box Seats In The Kingdom
Sermons For Pentecost (Last Third)
William G. Carter

First Lesson Set

Light In The Land Of Shadows
Sermons For Advent, Christmas And Epiphany
Harold C. Warlick, Jr.

Times Of Refreshing
Sermons For Lent and Easter
E. Carver McGriff

Lyrics For The Centuries
Sermons For Pentecost (First Third)
Arthur H. Kolsti

No Particular Place To Go
Sermons For Pentecost (Middle Third)
Timothy J. Smith

When Trouble Comes!
Sermons For Pentecost (Last Third)
Zan W. Holmes, Jr.